The Hive

The Hive

Poems by Susan Stewart

The University of Georgia Press
Athens and London

© 1987 by Susan Stewart
Published by the University of Georgia Press
Athens, Georgia 30602
All rights reserved
Designed by Betty P. McDaniel
Set in Palatino
The paper in this book meets the guidelines for
permanence and durability of the Committee on
Production Guidelines for Book Longevity of the
Council on Library Resources.

Printed in the United States of America

91 90 89 88 87   5 4 3 2 1

Library of Congress Cataloging in Publication Data

Stewart, Susan.
  The hive.

  I. Title.
PS3569.T474H5 1987   811'.54   86-19159
ISBN 0-8203-0918-4 (alk. paper)
ISBN 0-8203-0919-2 (pbk.: alk. paper)

British Library Cataloging in Publication Data
available.

for Jacob and Sam

Acknowledgments

The author and the publisher gratefully acknowledge the following publications in which poems for this volume first appeared, often in substantially different form.

American Poetry Review: "Life on Other Planets," "The Factory Girls Get Up to Read Shakespeare," "Seven Bridges"
Crazy Horse: "The Last Prince of Urbino"
Georgia Review: "Blue Willow"
Kayak: "Proverbs of the Sleeping Gypsy" (under the title, "The Sleeping Gypsy")
Memphis State Review: "Mouth of the Wolf," "In the Novel"
Missouri Review: "The Cardinal"
The Nation: "Gaville"
Poetry: "Man Dancing with a Baby," "Budapest, March 1928: The Genius of Friendship," "Fire Ceremony," "Consecration"
Poetry Northwest: "The Map of the World Confused with Its Territory," "Letter from Turin," "The Evening of Montale's Death"
Seneca Review: "The Summer Before the Moon," "André Derain: *Woman in Chemise,*" "A Garland"

"Man Dancing with a Baby," "The Evening of Montale's Death," "Consecration," and "Secret Ceremony: The Sailboat" appeared in *New American Poets of the 80's,* edited by Jack Myers and Roger Weingarten (Wampeter Press, 1984).

Completion of this manuscript was aided by grants from the National Endowment for the Arts, the Pennsylvania Council on the Arts, and Temple University.

"Budapest, March 1928: The Genius of Friendship," is for Edward Hirsch; "Gaville" is for the Halevy-Martini children; "The Last Prince of Urbino" is for Daniel Halevy. "Budapest, March 1928: The Genius of Friendship" is based on a photograph by Martin Munkacsi. The translation forming the epigraph is from Pier Paolo Pasolini, *Poems,* selected and translated by Norman MacAfee with Luciano Martinengo (New York: Vintage, 1982, p. 143).

Contents

Age, then, made
of my mother and me
two masks
that have lost nothing, though,
of morning's tenderness
—and the ancient rite
recurs
in its authentic form,
which only by dreaming inside a dream
could I perhaps call by its true name.

—*Pasolini*

I

Man Dancing with a Baby

Before balance, before counting, before
The record glistens and the needle slides,
Grating, into the overture, there is the end
Of weight, the leaning into nothing and then

A caught breath, the record listens, the needle slides
Over slowly, and all at once around us a woman's voice
Stretches weightless, leaning into nothing.
Like a clothesline, the taut chorus: oh, hilarious

Oh baby, all around us, over slowly, a woman's voice
Gathers above the pick me up, pick me up
And the desperate put, put me down. First the tightrope,
Then the light foot, and the taunting chorus

Pick me up, pick me up. Oh, oh baby.
The slippery floor shimmers and spins like a record while
The light is swinging footloose on its rope
Out of time. The shadows

Slip, shimmering black, and spin across the floor,
Then turn back and pick up again. Oh seedpod stuck for just
One moment on the cattail, out of time, out of shadows,
Downy cheek against a beard: oh scratches

On the record, oh baby, oh measure
Oh strange balance that grips us
On this side of the world.

Seven Bridges

Sometimes before I wake I see
an iron bridge reaching across a clear
line of tracks, a bridge that begins in blisters
and rust and arches away
into morning. Then I'm walking across
its sharp rails, and I feel its sway
and ripple, feel it like any inhuman thing

with a beginning and end and no middle.

Or it could be this bridge, half-drowned
in the Susquehanna, half-dead in the yellow water
and its pilings furred by moss. Then on the other

side, the devil bridge of Bagni di Lucca,
convulsing like an ingot in the blast
of a furnace before it lands, belly up
and steaming. Beyond that the false happiness

of the bridge to Camden or the six boards
nailed across the cow pasture's creek.
Downstream, the bridge I can't remember

like pairs of wings lifting over Mexico.

There always comes a point when I'm tired
of other sides and remember there was only
one bridge after all: the one by the olive oil plant
in Somerville, Massachusetts.
It made a faint music in the wind,
though I never crossed it in the morning
or in the evening, either.

Consecration

The man in the yellow hard hat,
the one with the mask
across his nose and mouth,

pulls the lever that turns
the great arm of the crane up
and over and sideways

toward the earth;
then the wrecking ball
dangles crazily,

so delicately, like a silver fob
loosened from a waistcoat pocket:
shocking to see

the dust fly up and the timber
sail up, then so slowly
down, how the summer air

bristles with a hundred splinters
and the smallest is a splintered flame,
for it takes so many lengthening

erratic movements to tear away
what stands between the sidewalk
and the bell tower,

where the pigeons now rise
in grand indignant waves
at such poor timing, such

a deaf ear toward the music;
in this way the silence

between hand and lever is turned
into a ragged and sorely lifted
wing: the wrecking ball lurches
in a narrowing arc until only

the dust resists—the rest
comes down, story by story,
and is hauled off in flatbed trucks.

Meanwhile the pedestrians come
and go, now and then glancing
at their accurate watches.

Gradually, the dust
becomes the rose light
of autumn.

But one evening a woman
loses her way as she's
swept into a passing wave

of commuters and she
looks up toward the perfectly
empty rectangle

now hanging between
the rutted mud and the sky.
There along the sides

of the adjacent building,
like a set for a simple
elementary school play,

like the gestures of the dead
in her children's faces,
she sees the flowered paper

of her parents' bedroom,
the pink stripes leading
up the stairs to the attic,

and the outline of the claw-
footed bathtub, font
of the lost cathedral of childhood.

A Garland

Care is heavy
therefore sleep you.
You are care and care
must keep you.
—Thomas Dekker's lullaby

1. THE ANNOUNCEMENT

Here are the four
posters of the bed, the four
angels circling, their wings
almost touching, and farther

The four corners
of the room, the roof,
the four steeples
and, beyond, the dark rim

Of the rain-slicked highway,
cut loose and circling
the square of the town.
This will be the earthly

Constellation of your birth.
But tonight, clouded cell,
first wing branching
into still water, tiny

Coral reef accruing
so faintly, so
purposefully, out of
nothing, tonight

The dead gather
in the empty hallway,
worrying their small
slips of paper, *no this*

*One, no that one, let
this one be the name.*

2. HARVEST HOME

*To dream of the living
and not the dead,*

*Sleep with a pale slip
over your head.*

Here was the house of plenty,
in October, a speckled
gourd split open,

Corn shocks tied
to the choir loft: *harvest home.*

A small girl sang
her solo so high you could see
it almost hurt.

There in the aisles
we built a holy wall

Meant to stand between
summer and winter;
on this side, the soup cans,

The spilling bushel baskets;
on the other, the invisible

Poor, the visible minister and
memory of thirst in the fields.
Those nights the moon, cut

From yellow paper, then attached
with straight pins

To the uncomplaining sky,
fell on that white house,
the silver maple, the button zinnias

Gone to seed.
Homemade world, bright paperweight . . .
the rain comes in the windows.

3. THE CEDAR TREE

Soon the rain turns to snow.
The stone animals,
Restored, have gathered
In the garden
Like punctuation marks
Someone has typed
Into a page,
And the places
Where we fell, arms
Spread, making angels,
Are distinct now,
Filling with the dusk's
Blue shadows.
A child, so happy with
The outline, often
Thus forgets the eyes
And mouth, as if
He could see straight through
To the soul
And the edge, once

Defined, were everything.
So it is tonight
That the other leaves
Are gone, then gone again
Under the winter's
Erasing, and the cedar
Huddles against your
Window, the only thing
Living above this earth.
Look how the new bark
Has sheathed the old
Dead tree, how
The outline, being
Everything, runs with
Golden sap, and although
The heartwood has seemed
To turn to stone,
How a single
Waxwing
Waits there.

4. FROZEN SPRING

Picture the way after twelve nights
the bean king springs

From his smooth cocoon;
a green flag,

Swatch of rag
from the cuff of winter, tearing.

Then the pencil-line
tendrils, the blind men

Revolting; we've made a rough lattice
to stand by the side.

The winding strands begin
their cool embrace of that ladder:

With what absolute
knowledge do they

Lay their hands upon it,
though it's dark and the stars, too,

Have let go of one another,
their lines and dots, once known

By heart, impossible to draw.

5. THE CROSSROADS

At the crossroads, as children,
we twisted the sign so that
it pointed from heaven to earth—
the fields of wheat, corn, oats,
and rye were the quadrants
of a country without name
or destination; yet this place,
we understood, had been the site
of a barn where someone
had been sheltered,
someone had been found, and
thus what might have passed
for accident or random
became a particular language
made from stones; the obsessive
needlework of hawks, in flight,
above us, the gradual
unfolding of a tented sky.
Oh sky that seemed to rise,
overnight, our mantle,
that we might sleep or go
on wandering, as we chose.

6. MOTHER'S DAY

If your mother is alive, wear
a red carnation; otherwise, wear
a white one to the banquet.
  —Mother's Day program, 1962

This was the black day in the house of straw,
The frail house built by the north-gone swallows.
All morning they beat sideways against the windows, hollowing
An old ache out of ice and putty, then the slow thaw
Of daylight on the spattered panes. What calls
Them to that spent light must be desire, and desire's own callow
Reflection: the lost wing, the fire gone out, the tallow
Hardening. This, love, is the nest that falls

In the back of the mind forever, where a mother
Is still alive, a song's not quite forgotten, and so turns
Back slowly in strings and twigs. I need a mended curtain,
A battered red carnation, a certain
Accompaniment to the end of winter as this high sun burns
On the glass, the white blanket; an extra wing, a tuck or gather.

7. CRIED:

cried in the night, pulling
in the whole body
of the night and then out

like a longshoreman working a dark rope
leading out to a relentless
and unforgiving weight

that was not shaped, but simply
the tendon of the sea;
and in the riot of the water

lay the burden of the water,

13

its weight, steadfast, rushing in to
surround us, to take

our cleaving shape, though I went to you gladly
with the green milk, the guttering
light.

Fire Ceremony

A girl called out to her horse,
called out in the October night
when the storm had ended.
She called out, wandering
through the brittle fields
where the corn was still dry
above the soft mud and the pumpkins.

Called out in the October night,
the siren moaned slowly, then rose
to a wail, yet far away as if
in another story's kingdom;
her father running out in
half-zippered trousers, her mother
shrouded in a cotton housecoat.

When the storm had ended,
an orange light stained
the sky above the meadow,
for the fire leaped up
like a half-spoken word, turned
into a myth with no place
of beginning.

She called out, wandering
closer to the woods, following
the creek's silver thread.
It wound between the deep oaks
like the end of childhood,
the way a flaw had been woven
in her mother's dark hair.

Then through the brittle fields
the wind came rustling,

carrying an animal fear;
the black calf with his damp nose
now dusted by ashes,
a spindly goat crazy in the heat.
The wind came up on its charred wings

To where the corn was still a dry
and broken path and the sparks
were a string of Chinese lanterns
bobbing above the barn. By dawn
the scarecrows had gathered
on the hill—stick figures, the curious
and unrelated crowd.

Above the soft mud and the pumpkins,
she could hear the rising siren
of the dogs; her mother running out
with a hen below each arm,
then her father stepping back
below the spinning eye,
the four hoofs flying
through the open hayloft.

The Summer Before the Moon

Began its pull, the wire fence scrawled
in loops across the meadow, a far rain
came slowly toward her; one foot, then a pause
and then the other like a stubborn bride
with no one to give her away. She could hear
the long veil sweep against the clover,
the smell of earth, everywhere, turning up its face.

And then it stopped, just beyond the reach
of the fence, as if a cloud had stepped back
like a startled deer, as if a door
had been closed so softly no one
noticed, although the other side would now
be understood as a different world.
This is how a child learns to wait for hours,

listening for something like a ceremony
to begin, something that as yet
has no name.

The Cardinal

It was on a day like this one.
The cardinal was in the mock orange bush,

Then gone. There was a spot of blood
left in the snow—the last exclamation
point of March.

Next door the policeman's wife
lifted her arms and turned

Once more, slowly, toward the wall.
A baby fell into a heap of dirty clothes.

Everywhere I heard the distant murmur
and laughter of televisions in vacant rooms.

I thought that my parents were sleeping,
that my sister had been thrashing
through a dream's black water.

There was a culvert in the thicket, then,
behind the schoolgrounds and it led

To a perfect circle of green.
This was the light that receded
as we ran our hands along the rippling

Metal sides, our necks bent slightly,
aching toward the water.

Turning back, I don't understand
anything, until years later
when it's too late

and something else, like this, has begun.

The Evening of Montale's Death

A green light trailed through the park at dusk
like a lantern slowly lifted
by a search party, but it was only

A fisherman starting out
to avenge some private grief.

Two by two, the couples hurried
into the inn with its dulled music of spoons
against linen. This was the first

Evening of autumn.
The dogwood smouldered at its edges;

Soon every shadow would be blazing
into the black winter rains.
This was the last summer evening; a mist fell

Softly on the benches and on the lightning-scarred faces
of the pine trees. What the sun had tried to make simple

The night was about to obscure.
Because out of that mist with its comings and goings,
its rich promise of darkness,

Rode all the particular errors of God:
the june bugs carrying their swollen bellies

On frail and pitiful wings, while above
the mulberry trees tried to hide
their aborted, patchwork leaves.

A pair of runners limped by with their arms thrown
around each other, and a small woman

In a large winter coat dragged
her wheel-less bicycle beside them.
There was a Boy Scout troop whose marching

Song was in the fabulous alphabet of the deaf,
and a man who swore over and over

To himself that he would never again
return. They all ran after the trailing
green light and toward the promise of winter,

Away from some sure place of beginning,
which one by one

They had neither remembered nor forgotten;
just as at dawn a search party
gathers in an open field

And a lantern is held up to each face
to be certain that nothing has changed.

II

Blue Willow

What does the boatman without oars on that
white stream? Who people the houses in that
charmed island?—or why do those disproportionate
doves forever kiss each other, as if intensely
joyful over some good deed done? Who is there
through whose mind such thoughts as these have
not passed, as he found his eye resting upon
the willow-pattern plates as they lay upon the
dinner-table, or brightly glittered on the cottage
plate-rail?
—The Family Friend, 1849

I

A woman grows up
in her father's house while
everything else stays the same.
Inside, a white cloth
is spread on the table with
the undeserved respect shown
the dead. The heavy doors
are locked into place,
one after the other; the sky
behind the grate, an appalling
ceramic blue.

II

It's true that the idea
of pure love depends
upon the cruelty of the father.
Last night I dreamed
of a paradise where the fences
were shuffled by the wind

and I gave each tree its
proper name: flowering cherry,
Chinese elm, the branch
that is broken by weeping.
The white gravel with its blank
upturned face; no one
could follow us there.

III

Out on the bay, I can see
a little houseboat. Its sails
are folded and it sleeps on
the waves so guiltlessly
a gull has built her nest
in the mast. Inside there is
a candle and an open book,
a piece of bread and a silver
knife. A frayed rope leads
to the icy anchor. That boat
is the farthest place
from my body.

IV

And the sea is so dark
all around me. Through the mist,
the servants of God
cross the bridge: one
with the rod and one with
the lantern, and the handmaiden
who carries the distaff.
A light goes out in the gatekeeper's
cottage and slowly
each village is extinguished.
But then the distaff spins

through the night like a comet
and the women start
from their beds.

V

I have filled the jewel box with
sand and pebbles, I've forgotten
the weight of your head in my hands.
Let me say again how I hate
those cooing doves; their awful
symmetry, so plump,
so sincere.
For their world continued
its happy course around us
like unnatural decorations
on a tomb, while the fear of love
pulled us toward the water
and held us—dark
anchor, with its flukes
and its barbarous crown.

Budapest, March 1928:
The Genius of Friendship

There was not so much terror then:
all in all, they had a little money,

A sweet life as plain
as a hedge sparrow,

A proverb, where the scrolls
of the white iron beds

Creaked at noon
from the delirious

Weight of mothers
and fathers. And no one,

Child or parent, had a reason
to cry out.

At supper, the lace cloth was freshly
starched, had been ironed

Between two smooth sheets
of brown paper.

In this photograph,
which itself is not brown

Or scorched or cracked,
but as glossy as it was

The day it rose
from a bath

Of chemicals and light,
more vision than memory,

Every woman in that neighborhood—
the rutted end of town—

Has assembled, leaning,
on the wrought-iron balcony,

Looking down toward a stray dog,
the brackwater ditches, a scattered

Handful of men in gray fedoras
but, most of all,

Is watching as two small girls,
in straight bangs and wildly

Polka-dotted dresses,
begin, with awkward

And painful concentration,
to dance a little forward,

A little back,
between the ditches

And the catcalls,
against the sheer

And dangerous weight
of the future,

Falling on that place.
I used to be so sure that

I was one of those two,
or perhaps both—

It doesn't matter—
but this morning

I remembered the missing part
of the picture

Where the flat brass lamp
sits, unreflecting,

On the table,
behind the dancers,

Behind the black balcony's
shadows, inscribing the starched

White aprons of the women—
the lamp that might

Be nothing if you say
we must compare it

To the random fireworks
of blood;

Yet whose poor, sufficient,
light does fall on our lives

And, when it does, is the seat
of the genius of friendship

Who conducts us from this world
and does not blame us.

Secret Ceremony: The Sailboat

There were thirty-six streets between us
and the moon and the weeds lay tangled,
the timothy broken off like a half-remembered

Song. I walked so slowly toward you,
toward the lights beyond the river,
but then the night came

Toward me and took away
my breath. What we meant to say:
how the seven stars assembled

Far above the vacant lot
where the tramps were burning paper,
gray boxes,

Bursting in the rusted
oil drum. That fire was forbidden,
yet they called out to a woman,

Pointed to the tangled moon;
she turned her head. The scene they never
show is the two of us

Pulling away, as the arms come down
untangled, like separate leaves
in November air, or a train

Circling forever beneath the high vault
of the station, a hand half-raised,
a look no one recalls.

Since that time I've seen

a small blue sailboat falling,
always, when I close my eyes.

What I meant to say:
how these are the flimsy
paper states,

the cardboard expanse
of a country without you;
how they flare up suddenly

from the stillness of the heart
like an oil spill—secret faces
in the surface of the river.

Letter from Turin

after Coleridge

Tonight the moon is falling like a piece of silver
into the black apron pocket of the sky

Then falling again as if some hidden hand
kept putting it back and taking it out—

Can you tell me, from there, does this
seem a mistake or the purest

Of repetitions? What I have learned
is the darkness in the daylight and the furnace

Of a strange machine: you cannot imagine
how the piston's hoofbeats can pound

Through my chest until dawn,
or how the oil slicks carry the illusions

Of nightfall;
you cannot imagine my face.

As I write, the brown grease swirls across
my palms and I am leaving you

The fingerprints of someone else's life.
The trolleys hover like a thousand

Angry bees and are the only animals for miles.
Once at noon I saw the light fall

On the haystacks and the vineyards,
but it was only a flowerpot in an office window;

The mountains in the doorway of the postcard shop
turned into a death mask of Verdi.

I have been to the cinema several times
to see the bareback riders of the West,

And a black man from America plays the saxophone
each night on the corner for cigarettes.

You ask about the hours I have to myself
and I answer they are only

The pauses of sleep; I open the courier
of evening for news, but its world

Is not my world—the girl who takes
it through the cafés does not at all

Resemble our daughter. I've seen her cross
the street like a small black leaf borne up

And around by the air. I move your photograph
each morning and evening from the wall

To my shirt and my shirt to the wall,
and hope that this letter is like money or luck;

First in one hand, then in another,
until all that remains is a soft shred of paper

At the bottom of your apron pocket one washday.

In the Novel

He described her mouth as *full of ashes*.
So when he kissed her finally
he was thinking about ashes

and the blacker rim just below
the edge of the ashtray,
and the faint dark rim that outlined her lips,

and the lips themselves, at the limit
of another darkness, farther
and far more interior.

Then the way the red,
paling, just outside those lines
caught fire and the pages caught

soon after that. Slowly at first,
but then all at once
at the scalloped brown corners of each;

like the ruff of an offended and darkening bird,
extended, then folded
in on itself; multiple,

stiffening, gone.

André Derain, *Woman in Chemise*

1.

In the dream of constantly changing
her clothes, she can't find
her own face.

2.

As when a mother, pulling
down a shirt, says "Oh
where's Z . . . Oh, *here*
she is."

3.

Then everything falls
into place except *her*
face with its orange light,
its shadowy context
that is the body itself and what
it knows of enfolding.

4.

The changing of clothes
starts again: a corduroy skirt
worn thin at the waistband,
a striped blouse ripped
at the sleeve, a black glove
neatly rolled into a blue

5.

The long slip, the short hem,
the laceless off-white shoe.

6.

She can't find where she is.
It's the middle of winter.
The portrait is hanging in Prague.

7.

She's gone out into the snow, the thick
white paint that's been smeared below
the stricken medieval steeples, the hidden
faces of the moon and the clocks.

8.

It's true, there is nothing
on her shoulders; she is saying
is this the fear of birth or encroachment?

9.

The mother says, "Oh so
many others seem to suffer
from this very same dream."

10.

This constantly changing
dark closet of hangers, at whose
service, whose mind, so bent
toward revision

The Commuter's Wife

He touched his collar.
The sky was full of fishtail clouds,
and the low blue gate
marked with an X
swung slowly, sprang
wildly, then
wavered, caught,
shut.

The Factory Girls Get Up to Read Shakespeare

At dawn a piece of ice snaps from the roof
and a gull flies up and over near the river;

You so rarely see one alone.

I thought I heard gunshots as the sun set
last night, but it was only the floes
as they began to move downstream
toward Boston or maybe the ocean.

For in March the brave and stupid skater
drowns and the wind sounds like thunder
in my sleep.

Walking home this time of year I always
let my hair loose and I'm filled with a different
kind of racket.

Do you remember the serenade outside the gates
at noon, the Greek boys singing oranges
four for a quarter? Or how each night we welcomed
the drunken songs, the concertinas,

How these small speeches break above the mill?

I'll read anything so long as there's some
Italy in it, or, just the same,
a little music. I took some red crêpe

Last week from the scrap box and made
a long Venetian mask with whiskers
like a fox! The other girls said,

"Where will you wear that?"
but it doesn't matter to me.

Now at five as I turn up the wick by the window
I see the lights moving at Sarah and Mary's.
It's hard to tell if they're dancing
toward me or away;

When it's misty the street is a lazy canal
or anywhere I've never been.
I'm happiest when we each take a part

And I don't mind being a mule or a man.
If I could fit a horse, or a forest,
in this room I would—

And a velvet curtain. For when the night
makes the shadow of a lion in the basin
I can almost play the violin.

I'd plan to start our meeting with an adagio
like waving water and I'd drown out the church bells
first and then the morning whistle.

I love those moments when a silence comes over
our voices and the pages seem to rustle

Like squares of Chinese silk.
We often think of you, Hannah, and the ways you loved
Ophelia; it's sometimes hard for three of us

To take up all the roles. And we remember
how before you left you crept into
the Lowell's garden, saying

the one white swan circling on that
tiny crystal pond and why she doesn't fly away
I'll never guess.

At the Font of Aretusa

Some things cannot follow:
the charcoal mask smudged
around the red unblinking eye

And the starched white taffeta
feathers of the swan

As once more, ruffling, unfurling,
she turns in the peacock-blue water,
is turned on the current

With the slow precision of any
mythological subject.

Above a hundred unfortunate copper coins
and the single wavering milfoil,
hidden now and then in the dense

Papyrus that fringes her three
small islands, she is seen

As a consequence, a coda, to a likely,
unlikely, story of lust and water,
separate, then violate

Through chasm and river and
reef; water alternately

Stained and clear, reviving,
polluting, male and female;
flowing, spiralling still, then

Clouding, arriving
at last at this final clarity.

This salt spring, invented at the limit
of Ortygia, where a dozen happy couples
peer and turn and listen

On the last day of January,
1983, two days before the almond trees,

Starting in the west, are reported
to burst into their double
white flowers, all at once—

that is, not in sequence.

III

Mouth of the Wolf

In my photograph of the Sphinx,
wearing black robes extended heavily
    like open bat wings, two men

as big as this pen point
    steady themselves
    on the bright side of His neck.

Each stretches a left arm
to the collarlike ridge that forms a pediment
    for the god's enormous head.

And though a shadow
    obscures him, it seems from
    this distance that the closer of the two

has held his right arm forward
with considerable eloquence toward what must
    have been the mysteriously

elevated position
    of the photographer.
    Yet this picture-taker has everything

in focus: the faces of the men,
the Pharaoh's delicate ear, the serrated mane,
    and even the far grains of sand

in the visible, though cut-off,
    triangle of the pyramids, making up
    what could be called the background.

The shadowed, more bulbous

side of the headdress casts a mark to His left
in a patch of over-exposed sand.

This mark is confusing,
shallow or deep, a point
of absorption or an afterthought—

like a cavernous, yet
silent, and displaced mouth.
In other words,

what rain there is
can be found in this shadow's
shadow. The rain which falls

alike upon every country,
and the other rain, too, which disappears
from the picture.

Life on Other Planets

campo dei fiori

Nothing so heretical as dusk—
the softened flesh of the peaches giving way
under their split panne skins

and the sepals of the harvested
Madonna lilies beading with
a sudden, sexual honey;

things opening and closing by
foregone equations: the clock tower
or this boy's spilling accordion,

the shape of a quarter note emptied,
then full-measured, beside the glossy
olives and salt-silvered fish.

Here at the center of this zodiac
of plenty stands Bruno's statue
at the site of his burning,

his black cowl restored, the articulated
folds now stolid, cold;
the city's pith.

Yet nothing in this age so heretical
as dusk, washing over the square
with its simple confusions—

number, name, the shifted heavens,
now opening shadows, now closing flames.
For if there are flowers on this

paved earth, why not flowers

on another and others
in our likeness—fallen,

threshed, in a field in late September
and the field itself falling
through the near-guess of night?

The Map of the World Confused with Its Territory

In a drawer I found a map of the world,
folded into eighths and then once again
and each country bore the wrong name because
the map of the world is an orphanage.

The edges of the earth had a margin
as frayed as the hem of the falling night
and a crease moved down toward the center of
the earth, halving the identical stars.

Every river ran with its thin blue
brother out from the heart of a country:
there cedars twisted toward the southern sky
and reeds plumed eastward like an augur's pens.

No dates on the wrinkles of that broad face,
no slow grinding of mountains and sand, for—
all at once, like a knife on a whetstone—
the map of the world spoke in snakes and tongues.

The hard-topped roads of the western suburbs
and the distant lights of the capitol
each pull away from the yellowed beaches
and step into the lost sea of daybreak.

The map of the world is a canvas turning
away from the painter's ink-stained hands
while the pigments cake in their little glass
jars and the brushes grow stiff with forgetting.

There is no model, shy and half-undressed,
no open window and flickering lamp,
yet someone has left this sealed blue letter,
this gypsy's bandana on the darkening

Table, each corner held down by a conch
shell. What does the body remember at
dusk? That the palms of the hands are a map
of the world, erased and drawn again and

Again, then covered with rivers and earth.

Proverbs of the Sleeping Gypsy

When the animal eye of the moon hangs above us
the earth, our instrument, comforts us below.

*

Joseph's brothers grew fond of the autumn
and thought of trees
as *those which do not flower.*

*

A striped curtain is not a prison; a flowered curtain
is not Paradise.

*

Sandy lake: sea on fire:: hickory wood for the gypsy's bier.

*

An aluminum arrow lightens the clock; time is proven through
the changes in metals.

*

Remember the error of Joseph's brothers.

*

The wife will say there is no one in your life:
the husband will say you must certainly die.

*

The Queen of Persia rose bears a bitter fragrance;
the moss rose wears the sweetest thorn.

*

A stone house will never be empty.

*

First snow, best for bread: last snow,
best for chaff.

*

Language, our amulet: dancing, our element.

*

If you come back when you are not expected,
do not stand freely in the eyes of women.

*

A bad check, a sidelong gaze; this is how
the wagon rope frays.

Gaville

The other was he because of whom
you, Gaville, weep
—Canto XXV, *The Inferno*

At evening the laundry
sags from each window, gaudy and
blushed by the rain, while the happy old Communist
in the hospital corset nails up a notice
of another picnic.

So many bees circling
in and out of the hive and the grapes
nodding heavily on their gray-green vines: olive
branches, doves, the buff sheets of
someone's dowry—before you

Lie all the standard
paraphernalia of peace. The bocce ball
misfires, angles down the hill, and fades into
the orchard's fretwork shadows.
If all the evil in the world

Fell into this place:
if the Cavalcantis rode again on their
furious stallions and the newborns were silenced
in their cribs: or say the Germans
returned, marching through

The wheat, and shot
whatever moved, and set fire to
the oleanders; if the power plant started its
relentless blows and the rain itself
invented a newer, sharper

Needle, what remained
would begin again. The children would
still take up jogging. The coach with the tumor
would still hold the stopwatch. The bocce
ball would roll back,

As in a movie, when
the snow melts and the oleanders
flame into bloom. And each evening would come
in on the yellow air like this one,
like a lost bee that never

Knew what smoke means:
how something burns always once the hive
has been destroyed.

Eight Tableaus of a Rumor of War

1 .

The raven fell from a shadow on the sun
and landed like a blow on the lawn.

2 .

That day, by the river, the workmen
fished out a horse; the rope heaved slack
and taut, slack and taut,
almost a kind of breathing,
but in the end there was only
the swollen hide with its rolling hills,
its hundreds of miniature waterfalls.

3 .

The raven's wing was soft against our cheeks
and the quills could be bent without breaking.

4 .

A boy bought a pistol at a fair
in the suburbs; he counted out the pennies
like small copper slugs.
When his younger brother let go
of the heart-shaped balloon, it flew
into the arms of The Crazy Saucer.

5.

Their mother's black hair was brushed up into
a wing and held in place
by a silver clip that caught the sun.

6.

The arsonist set fire to the church
with the altar candles themselves.
He moved from left to right,
cushion to hymnal, and then threw
the soft wax into the snow.
The report of the inspector went on
for many pages, yet where he meant
to write *thief*, he wrote *alterboy*,
and where he meant to write
snow, he wrote *letter*.

7.

The raven's wing swept against
the sky and left a print, a deep
and liquid stain.

8.

After years, the killdeers came back
like the mended pieces of a long brown ribbon;
their songs wound all around the house
until we could bear them no longer.
A man pulled away from a woman
at that time and a child brought
tremendous news home from school.

The Last Prince of Urbino

1. BAROCCI, 1605

Before the skull closes, month by month,
the way the shape of a life comes closer

To itself until one morning
nothing will ever change again;

And before the eyes, irrevocably blue
and black, decide to stay blue

Or, seeing a vineyard, turn brown
or green or amber; before

The slow evolving of the body,
almost as automatic as forgetting

Or remembering, there are two
soft spots: one above the lovely pale

Arch of the forehead and the other,
farther back, at the top of the crown,

Hidden in the faint shadow of hair
which, called *lanugo,*

First covers the body entirely and then
recedes into the places of ornament

And secrets--twin nests,
little swamps, between what's

Right and what's left and the beginning
of difference: matter, water, air.

For example, Barocci, homesick and out of date,
painted the newborn prince of Urbino

All black eyes and soft skull against
the gilt-embroidered pillow, knowing

That the limbs were perfectly common,
and so hid them inside a brilliant

Swaddling cloth that had ruined the sight
of a hundred maids-in-waiting.

For nine months a fortune in silver needles
wove blue and gold silk

Through the filmy linen, as if the sky
and sun could lend weight

To the air, the surface of things being
a kind of armor.

And the people, who long had yelled,
"Your Highness, take a wife,"

Were overjoyed that the world
they knew as this one might

Continue and that the body, clothed
in more than splendor from birth,

Could become the pure promise of spirit.
The end of the Renaissance, the rise

Of desperation. The Duchess made a pilgrimage
to the Madonna of Loreto: offering

The Virgin a golden plate, she slowly
uncovered the limbs of the child.

There were twelve young men at the gates
of Urbino, wearing cloaks of blue damask

Trimmed with gold, and twenty-four children
in gold and white robes: a book of hours

On the night she returned. They carried
the infant in a chair decked with fountains

And angels through the streets
to the palace. Almost two,

He faced Barocci with a tiny sparrow,
half in and half out of his uplifted fist,

The wings extended, then suddenly stopped
and a soft bruise appearing on the breast.

Another picture, at two, with a paddle
and ball (yet so dark it seems the painter,

Pressed by time, has wakened
the dreamy child to pose by candlelight).

This is all we know from the paintings:
Barocci dead, his pupil gone to Naples.

At four the prince was promised
to a Medici princess: she sent him a pony,

A poodle taught to leap, a jack-
daw, and, so that he might not

Forget the Scriptures, an inkstand
in the form of Mount Calvary.

In the carnival of 1617 nine couples of knights
fought within a barrier where two chariots raced,

one of Pallas and one of Venus.
The next year a wild boar, caught near Mondolfo,

was baited in the palace yard
with large dogs and spears.

The prince married the princess
and the people rejoiced. His ambition:

The revival of Comedy.
The night before his death, he played

A packhorse on the stage, all loose limbs
and sackcloth mane.

At daybreak, his servants came
into the room, crying, "Up, it's time

For the comedy," found the temples crushed,
the left hand open and extended,

One leg drawn high against the chest.
The old Duke, deeding his lands to the Pope,

Retired to a monastery, surrounded by
orange trees, the shoots of which had come,

Miraculously, from China. He wrote
in his diary: *so heavy*

And golden, so softly the fruit falls,
yielding, while I sleep.

2. JOSEPH CORNELL, 1967

Eddie Moss, 10, 240 Rose Street:
Eddie was with several members of his family
as they were driving to the White Castle
for dinner early Friday evening. When his
father, who was driving, saw barricades
on Elizabeth Avenue near the White Castle,
he slowed to a halt. National Guardsmen
opened fire. Moss then drove around the
barricades, stopped to let Eddie's uncle
jump out to wave down the Guardsmen,
then with Eddie's uncle back in the car,
drove away to escape further gunfire.
When they returned to their neighborhood,
the car was riddled with bullets and Eddie
was fatally wounded in the head.
—Tom Hayden, *Rebellion in Newark.*

Little one in the foreground,
The sky was on fire, at the vanishing
Point the ladybugs were flying
Home: the trees were turning

Black, black clouds were
Drifting quickly, through
The dusk, a wall of wind,
Now in smoke, now in flames.

Two cities were burning and
The people assembled, the ladybugs
Alighted, then *fly away, fly;*
Bricks in the air, sparks that

Rose so softly, window
Screens that fell so slowly

From the belly of the heat;
A spark, and the night

Put on its tarnished armor,
A kitchen knife tumbled
From a sky-blue drawer.
Little one, there was a war

Going on in the background,
The sky was full of roses
And their heavy lips were
Parted; a cloth draped every

Mirror; every hospital closed.
The sky was full of thorns and
The people assembled, someone shouted
So much glass in the corridors

Of night. Someone answered, sore
Afraid, and then the glass was shattered,
Shattered in sequence almost
Like evening chimes. And in

The distance, we could hear
The soft slap of the jump rope
As it rose and fell, so white,
So sharply through the darkness.

In the distance, we could
See the tower of the Castle,
A piece of black lace floating
From a mullioned window.

Ladybug fly away
For the hours were on fire
Your children are burning,
The clothesline was stolen

Then the curtains were flapping
From the windows—ragged flags,
Declaring no allegiance,
No sequence, children sobbing

Both hands pressed to the face, each
Back pressed to a skirt and
The skirts were flowering. No,
No mother flying, no mother

At home: for the houses
Were on fire, the children
Were burning, black clouds in
Every mirror and the doors

Torn from their hinges;
Still the people assembled
Like a harvest of leaves.
And a harsh light fell upon them,

Fell heavy as thunder: still
They did not scatter, though
The wind took on a body.
Little one, it was the body

Of hounds and fearful birds.
And then a red sky, reddening,
Sailor's delight. Little one, give
Warning, the sky was on fire.

Death to the Wolf

What can you recall?
     the traffic, pausing . . .
          owl, no, dove, no, one red
          finch left. A cry so human, why
               didn't anyone wake?

What else?
     Later a cloud
          wrested free of the moon, drifted
          toward the paler, eastern side of the city;
               how each night the morning
               reached back into the darkness—
                    desperate, but not confused, more
                    like the unborn than—

Who was there?
     no one. I didn't see anyone
          coming out or going in or in
          windows—though, fireflies
               in the yews like flecks of mica—
               those children . . . were they lifting
                    radios or ormers? Earlier, later,
               no one was there

What was it? What more?
     purely, yes, ordinary;
          I really couldn't,
          myself, see.
               By the solstice, it was finished,
               there and then; briefest night.

The Contemporary Poetry Series

EDITED BY PAUL ZIMMER

Dannie Abse, *One-Legged on Ice*
Gerald Barrax, *An Audience of One*
Tony Connor, *New and Selected Poems*
Franz Douskey, *Rowing Across the Dark*
Lynn Emanuel, *Hotel Fiesta*
John Engels, *Vivaldi in Early Fall*
John Engels, *Weather-Fear: New and Selected Poems, 1958–1982*
Brendan Galvin, *Atlantic Flyway*
Brendan Galvin, *Winter Oysters*
Michael Heffernan, *The Cry of Oliver Hardy*
Michael Heffernan, *To the Wreakers of Havoc*
Conrad Hilberry, *The Moon Seen as a Slice of Pineapple*
X. J. Kennedy, *Cross Ties*
Caroline Knox, *The House Party*
Gary Margolis, *The Day We Still Stand Here*
Michael Pettit, *American Light*
Bin Ramke, *White Monkeys*
J. W. Rivers, *Proud and on My Feet*
Laurie Sheck, *Amaranth*
Myra Sklarew, *The Science of Goodbyes*
Marcia Southwick, *The Night Won't Save Anyone*
Mary Swander, *Succession*
Bruce Weigl, *The Monkey Wars*
Paul Zarzyski, *The Make-Up of Ice*

The Contemporary Poetry Series

EDITED BY BIN RAMKE